WHO WAS CHRISTOPHER COLUMBUS? BIOGRAPHY FOR KIDS 6-8

Children's Biography Books

BABY PROFESSOR
EDUCATION KIDS

Speedy Publishing LLC

40 E. Main St. #1156

Newark, DE 19711

www.speedypublishing.com

Copyright 2017

All Rights reserved. No part of this book may be reproduced or used in any way or form or by any means whether electronic or mechanical, this means that you cannot record or photocopy any material ideas or tips that are provided in this book.

There's a verse that starts "In fourteen hundred and ninety-two / Columbus sailed the ocean blue..." Who was Christopher Columbus? Where did he sail to and what did he do there? Read on and find out!

FIRST VOYAGES

Christopher Columbus was born in 1451 in Italy. His father was a weaver, but other families members were involved in trading by ship. He started going on trading voyages with them when he was a teenager, and started to learn about the life at sea and how to sail a ship.

Christopher Columbus

Mediterranean Sea

In 1476 Columbus sailed out of the Mediterranean Sea and into the Atlantic Ocean for the first time. It was almost his last time! French ships attacked the trading fleet he was part of and burned his ship. He barely made it to shore in Portugal.

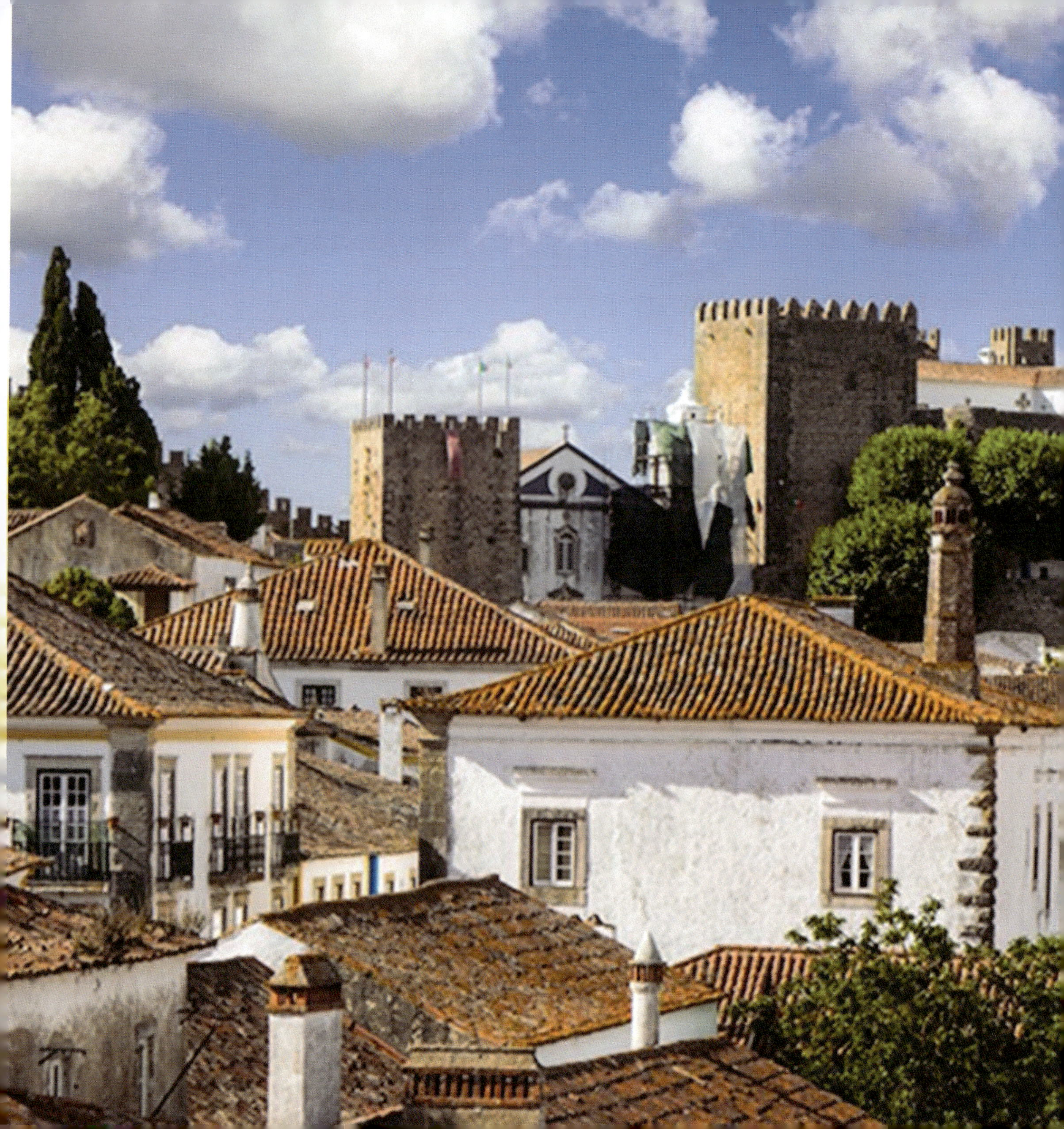

Columbus settled in Portugal, and later moved to Spain. He continued to take part in trading missions, learning about the Atlantic Ocean during trips along the African coast.

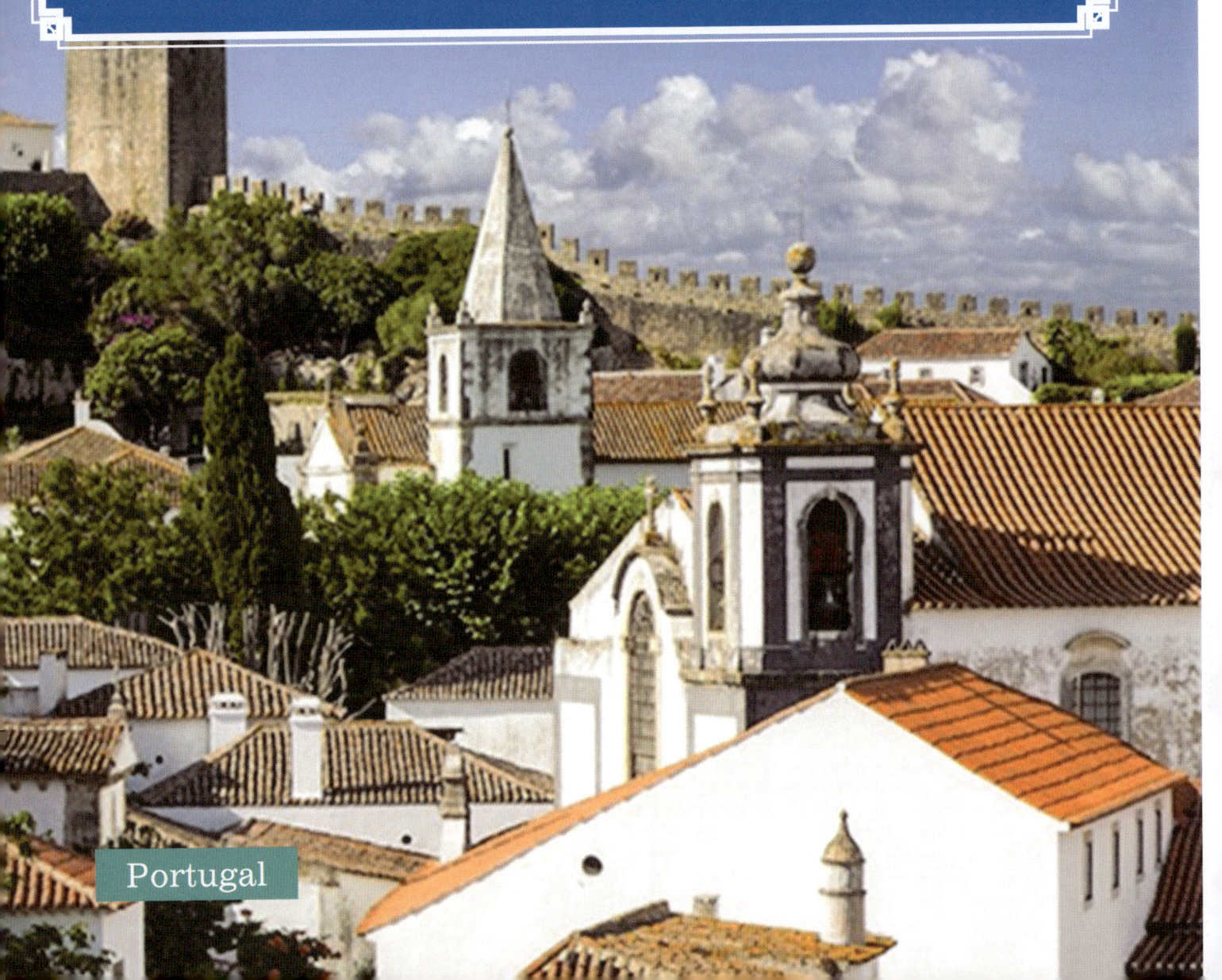

Portugal

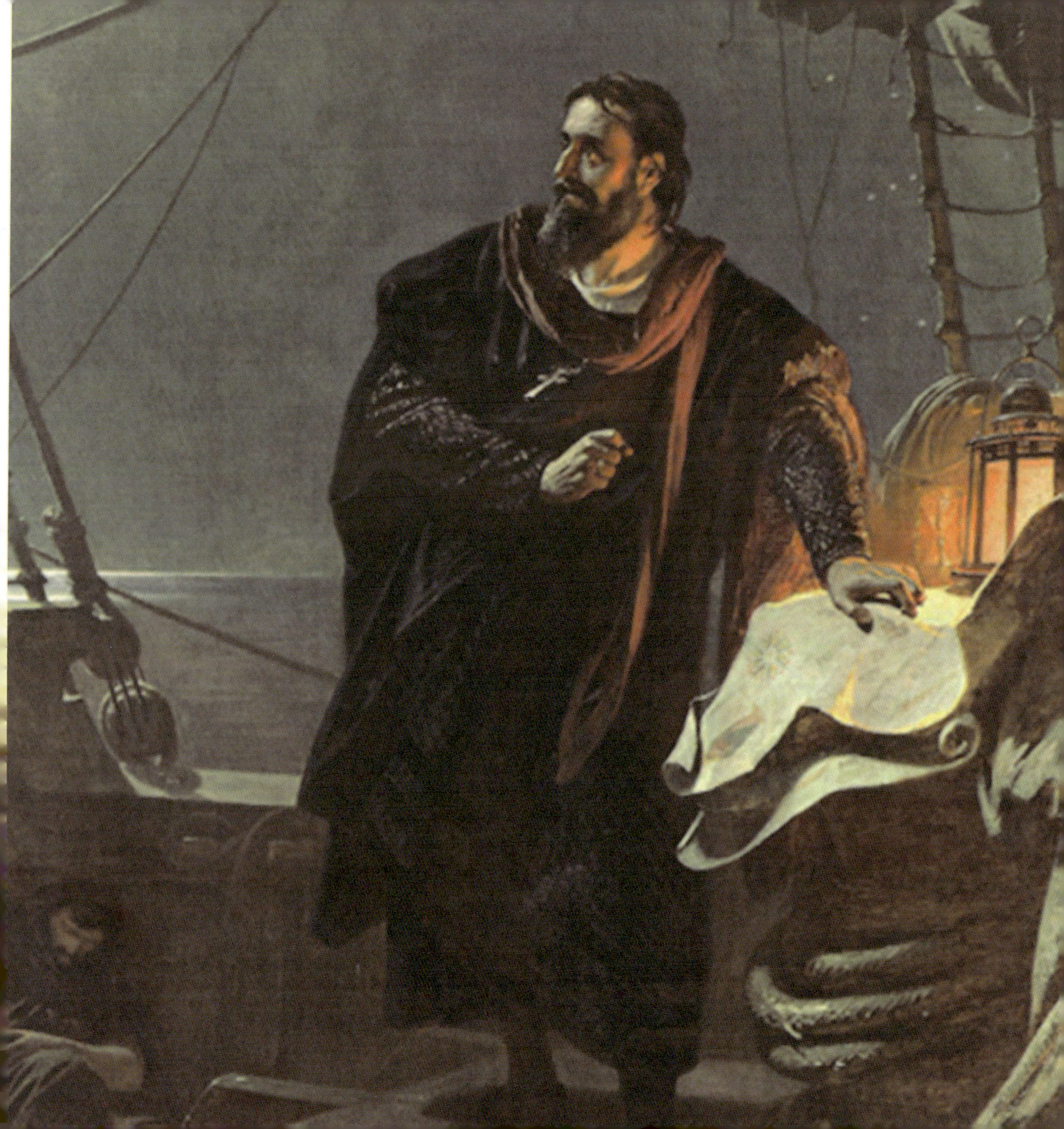

A NEW ROUTE TO THE FAR EAST?

Muslim countries controlled most trade between Europe and the Far East at this time, as all ships had to sail east through the Mediterranean and into areas of Muslim control before traders could continue to India and China. Going south around Africa was possible, but it was a long and dangerous trip.

Columbus came up with a plan to sail west to get to the east! Since he knew that the Earth is a globe, he thought it would be quicker, less dangerous, and less expensive to sail west from Europe to get to China.

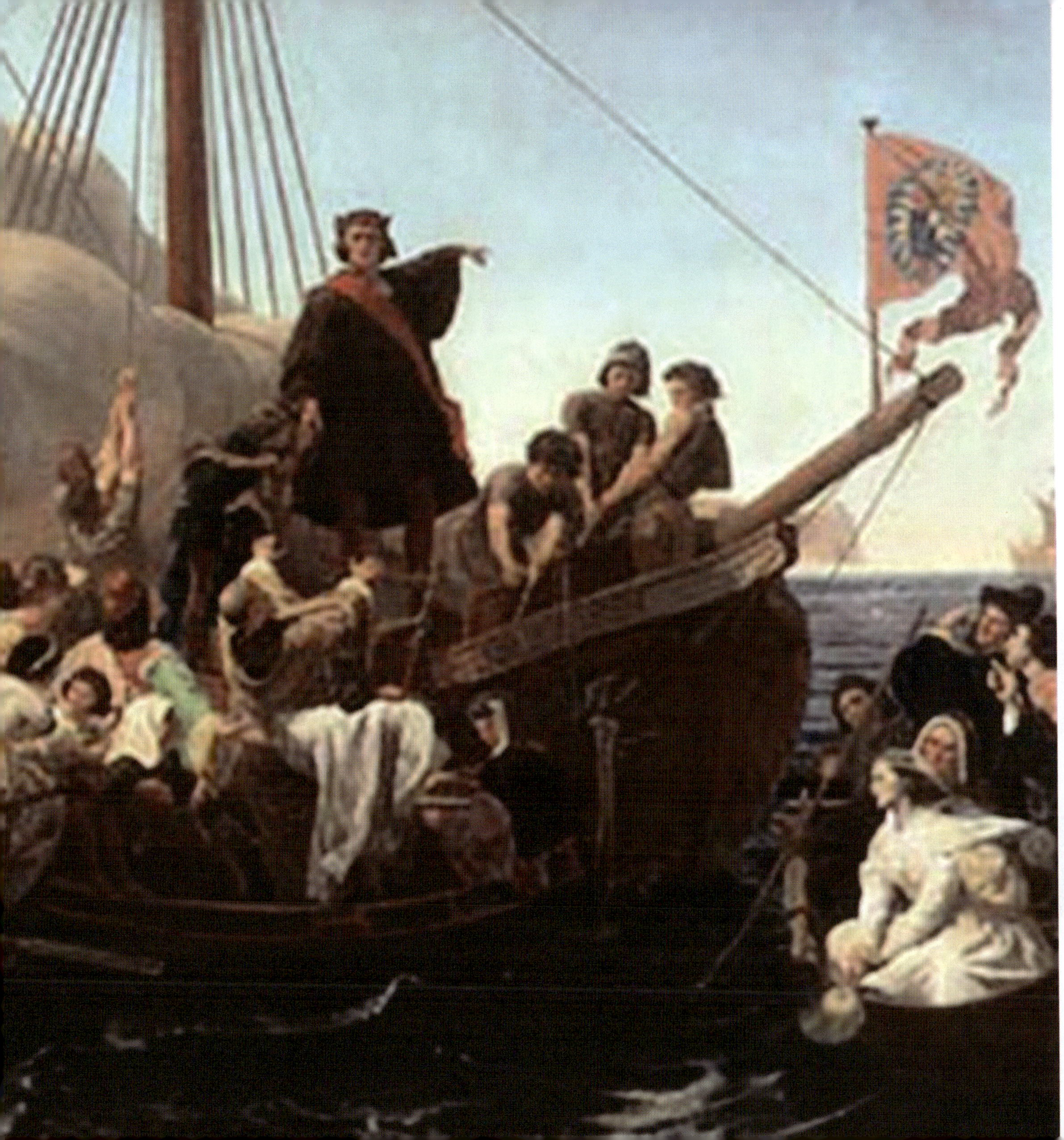

Canary Islands

In making this plan, Columbus calculated that the Earth was only about two-thirds as large as it actually is. He thought the distance by sea from the Canary Islands, off the west coast of Europe, to Japan would be less than 2,500 miles. It is actually more than 12,000 miles! Columbus made this mistake in part because he misunderstood a measurement on Muslim charts. He also trusted the reports of Marco Polo, who made China seem much larger than it is.

Christopher Columbus

At this time few people in Europe knew that North and South America lay between Europe and the Far East, even though fishermen from Portugal, Spain, France, and other countries had been fishing off the coast of Newfoundland

Newfoundland

and what is now Canada for many years. Columbus, and even the people who thought his estimate of the distance was wrong, all thought he had open ocean between Europe and the Far East.

Christopher Columbus

Columbus asked the king of Portugal to finance a trip involving three ships, and the king refused. The cities of Genoa and Venice also rejected the idea. The governments of Castille and Aragon rejected the plan as well in 1486, as they were in the middle of a war to conquer the Muslim part of what is now Spain.

When Spain was united as a Christian country in 1492, it paid for ships and supplies for Columbus to make his journey. He sailed with three ships, the Santa Maria, the Nina (named after its owner, Juan Nino), and the Pinta (a nickname meaning "the painted lady").

The Santa Maria at Sea

Bahamas

DISCOVERING THE NEW WORLD

After sailing west for 36 days, the expedition reached one of the islands in the Bahamas. They claimed it for Spain. They traded with the natives who lived there, and then continued west. Columbus was sure they were among islands near the coast of China.

One of the three ships was wrecked near Hispaniola, the island where Haiti and the Dominican Republic now are. Columbus and his men used wood from the shipwreck to build some simple houses, and thirty-nine of the crew stayed in the settlement while Columbus sailed home with the rest of the men in the two remaining ships.

Columbus Landing on Hispaniola

Hispaniola

FURTHER VOYAGES

Columbus reported back to Spain in 1493 that he had found the way to the riches of China. He sailed again later in the year and visited more islands in the Caribbean.

However, when he returned to Hispaniola, he found the little settlement destroyed and all its men killed or vanished.

Columbus was convinced that there were great riches, especially gold, in this new land. He forced the native people to rebuild the settlement and to hunt for gold for him, killing those who would not cooperate. He also viewed the native people as a very profitable source of slaves. He did not think of them as human beings like Europeans, but like lesser creatures who could be bought and sold.

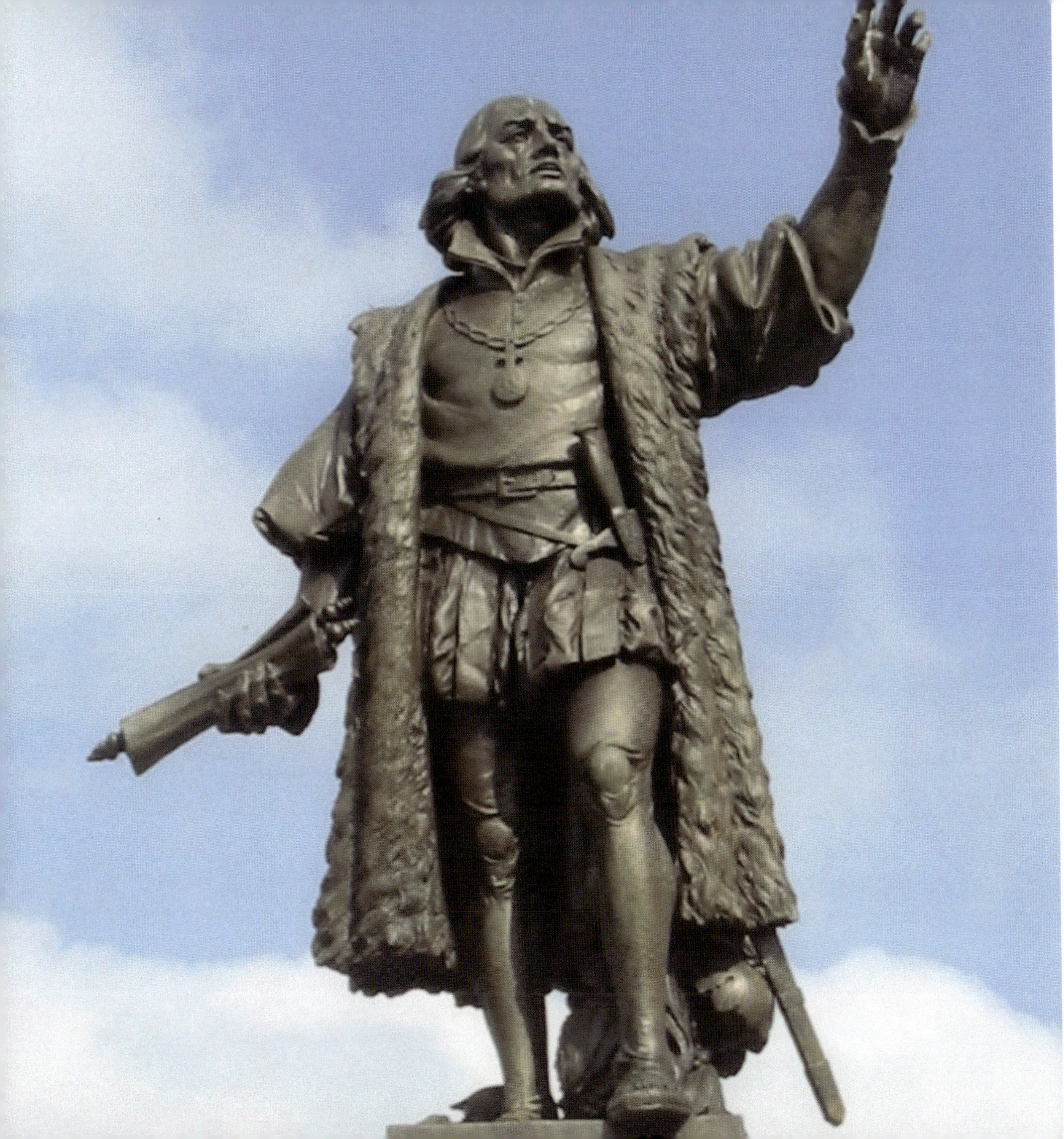

Columbus Landing in America

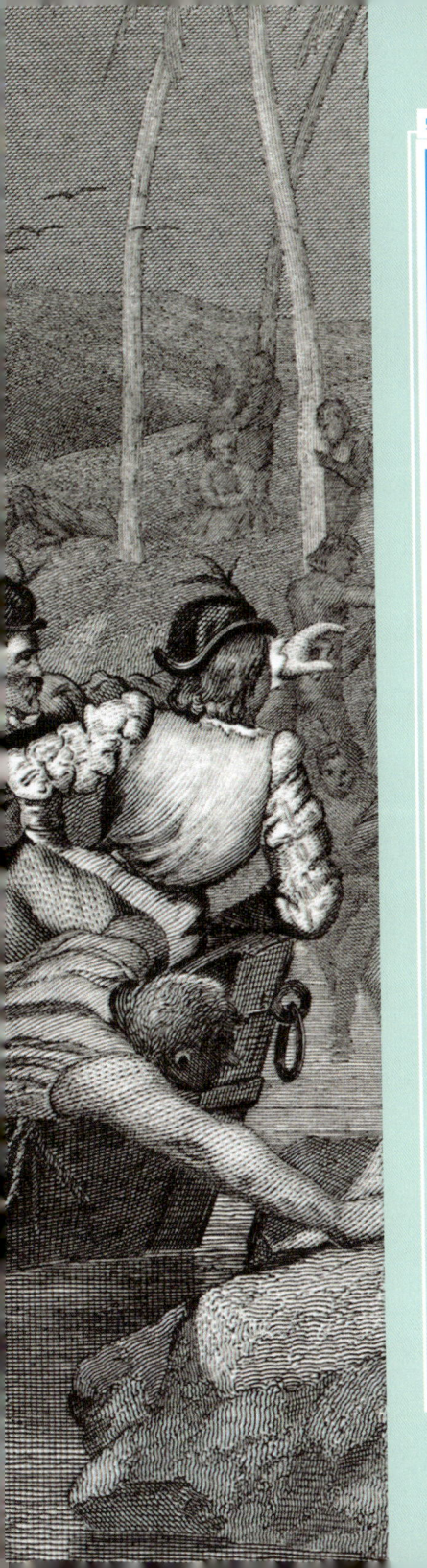

On his third voyage, Columbus finally reached the mainland of South America, at what is now Venezuela. However, he had found no gold, no great cities, and no wondrous cultures such as those Marco Polo had described.

His followers were near to mutiny, claiming that Columbus had lied to them about the riches they would gain, and upset about their living conditions. The native people hated and feared the Europeans by now.

Reports of unrest and failure made their way back to Spain. The Spanish government sent officials to arrest Columbus and bring him back for trial. All his wealth was seized.

Christopher Columbus Statue

Eventually the charges against Columbus were dropped and he regained some of his money. He convinced the king to let him make one more trip, on which he would find a way through the islands to the mainland of China.

Columbus sailed on his last voyage on 1502. His ship was wrecked on the coast of Cuba, stranding the expedition. The native people would not cooperate with the Europeans, who had been so cruel to them, until Columbus tricked them.

He knew from an almanac that there would be an eclipse of the sun, so he told the native people that he would take away their daylight unless they traded with him. The native people were convinced of Columbus' power and provided his expedition with food until they could be rescued.

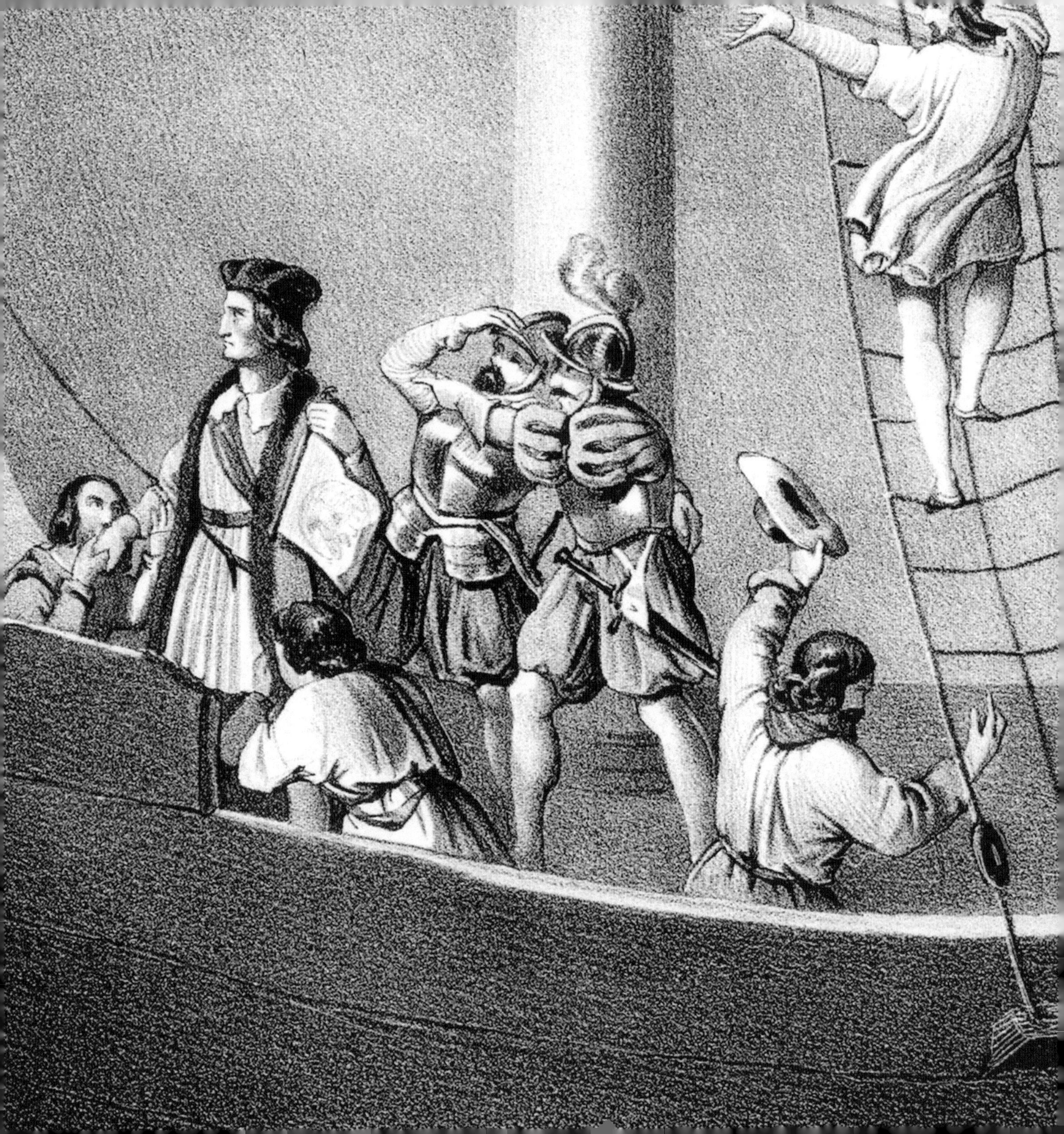

Columbus, King Ferdinand and Queen Isabella

COLUMBUS' LAST YEARS

Columbus made it back to Spain in 1504. No longer in control of Spanish efforts in the Caribbean. He lived for two more years, and spent most of that time arguing with the Spanish government to try to get the return of his wealth and some of his titles. When he died in 1506, aged 55, he still believed that he had found a short, easy route to the Far East.

THE LEGACY OF COLUMBUS

Columbus was a great navigator and made some remarkable discoveries, but he also opened the way to many bad things that Europeans brought to the native peoples of the Americas.

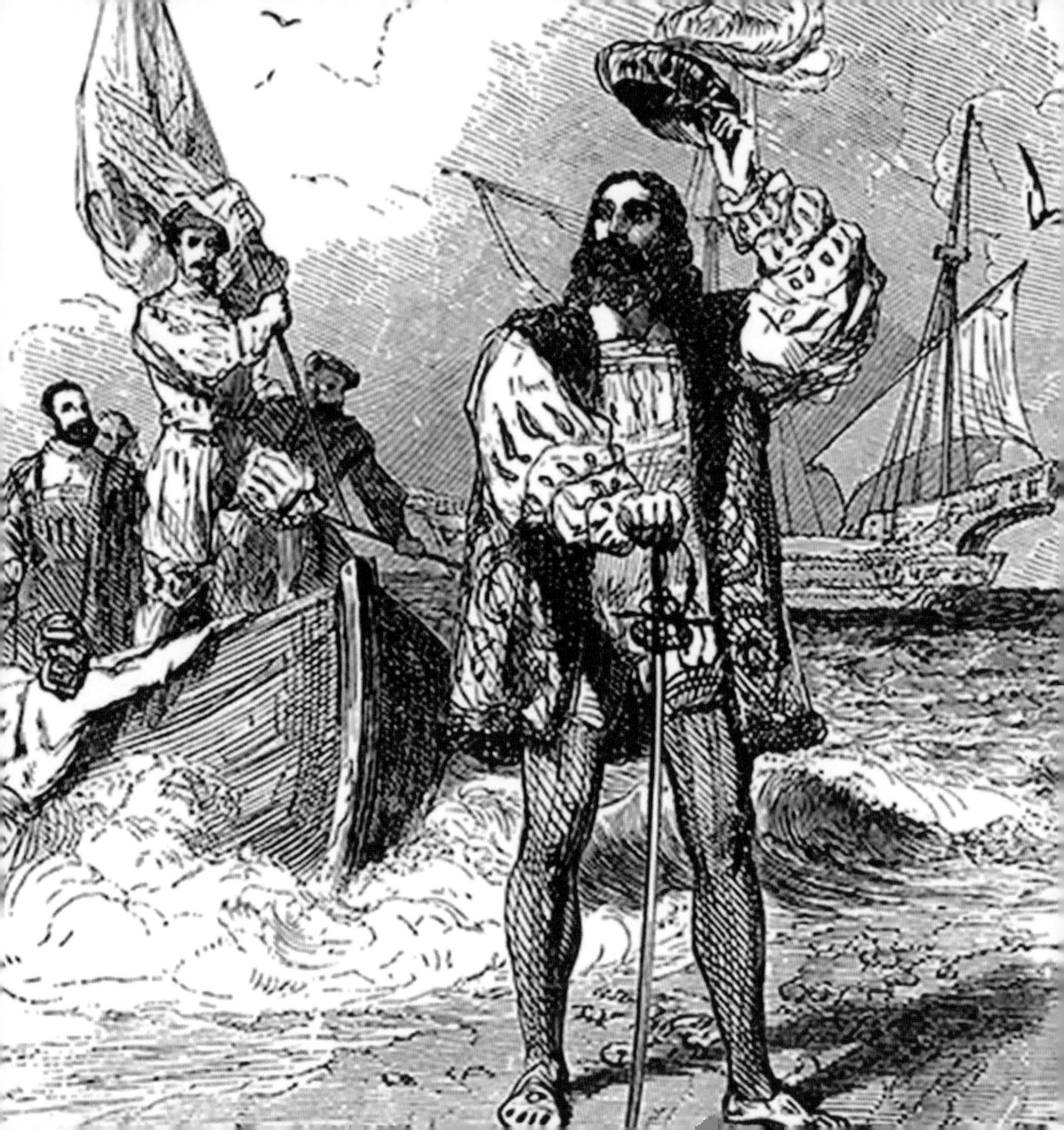

Columbus Monument in Spain

Columbus failed to find the route he had looked for, an easy way to the Far East, but he had found a whole New World that the governments of Europe had not known existed. This began the age of colonization and exploitation of both North and South America.

He brought back new plants, animals, and captive people to amaze the people of Europe and excite their imaginations. But he and his crew also brought diseases against which the people of the New World had no defenses.

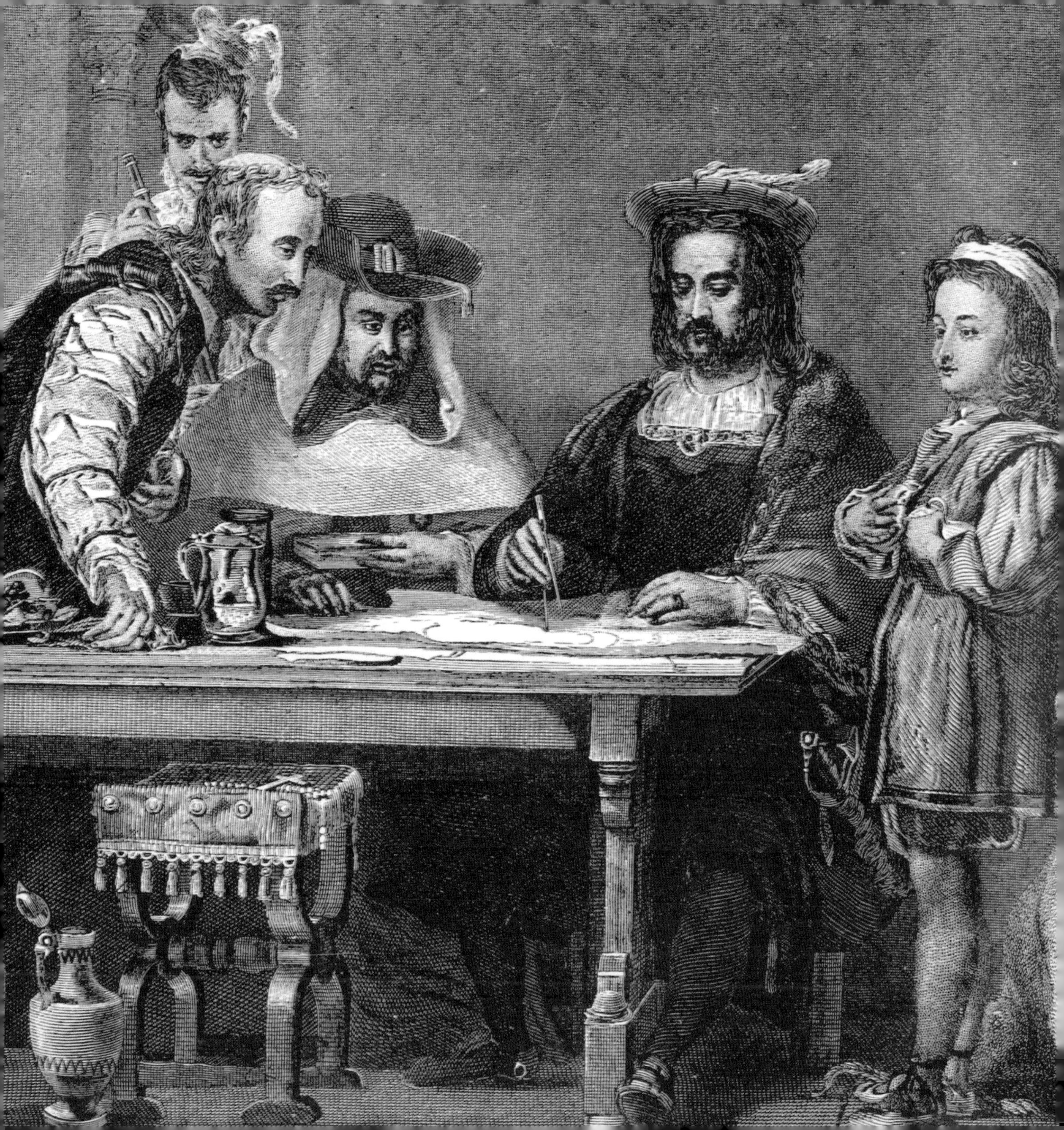

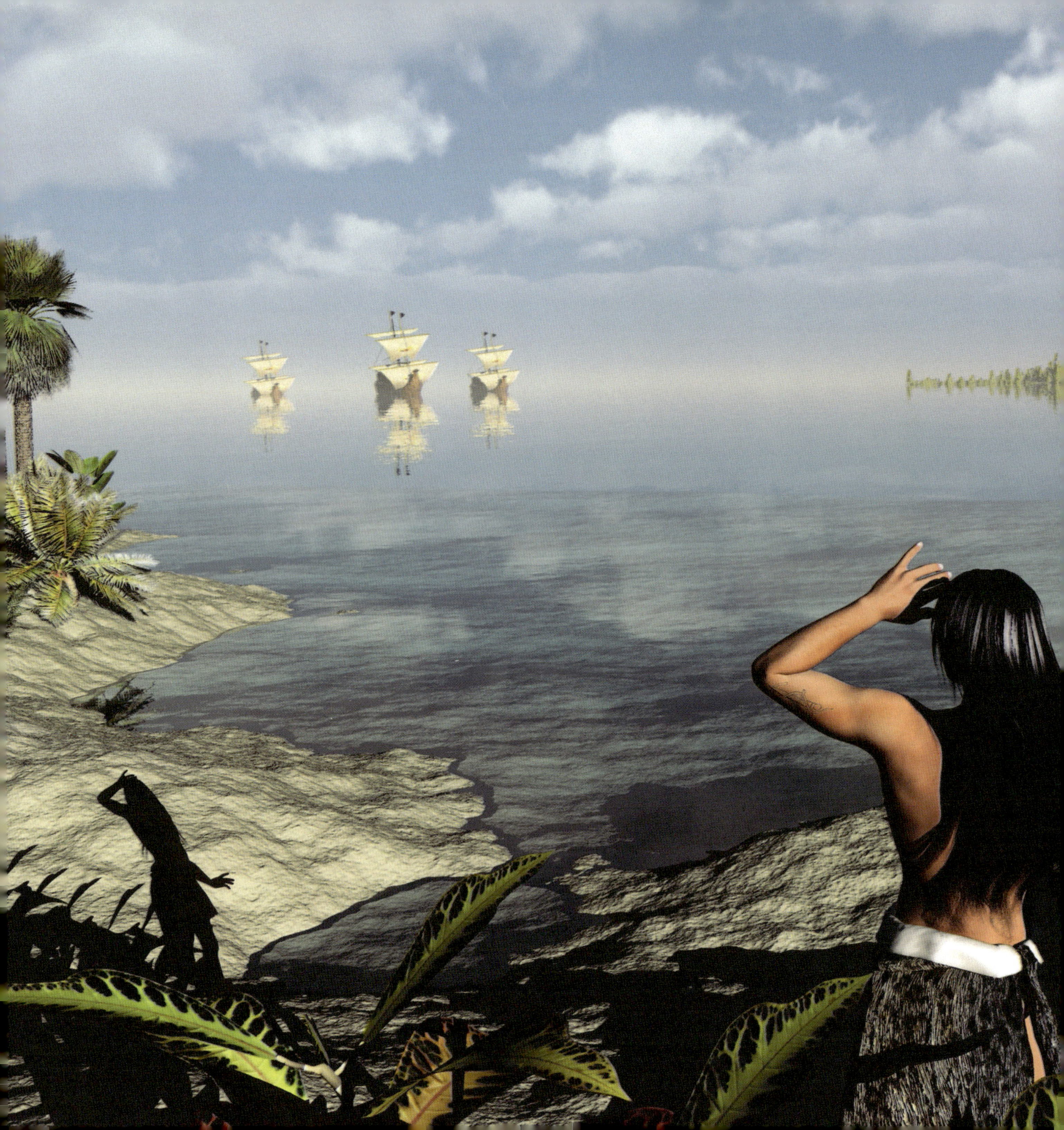

Millions of Native Americans died from diseases like measles, smallpox, and plague. This made the New World look like a gift from God to the Europeans, an empty Garden of Eden ripe for conquering.

Over time, the "Columbian Exchange" changed both the New World and the Old One. Europeans brought horses and crops like wheat to the new world, dramatically changing Native American cultures. New World plants like potatoes, tomatoes, and corn soon became essential to the European diet and economy.

Landing of Columbus

Christopher Columbus and Native American Men

Tobacco came from the New World to become a major diversion and addiction in the Old World. Over time, crops like African coffee and Asian sugar cane became major crops in the New World.

Because so many Native Americans died from European diseases, the Europeans started importing African slaves to work the plantation and hunt for gold. This was the start of the horrible slave trade that supported the economy at a tragic cost of human life for over three hundred years.

Columbus Discovering America

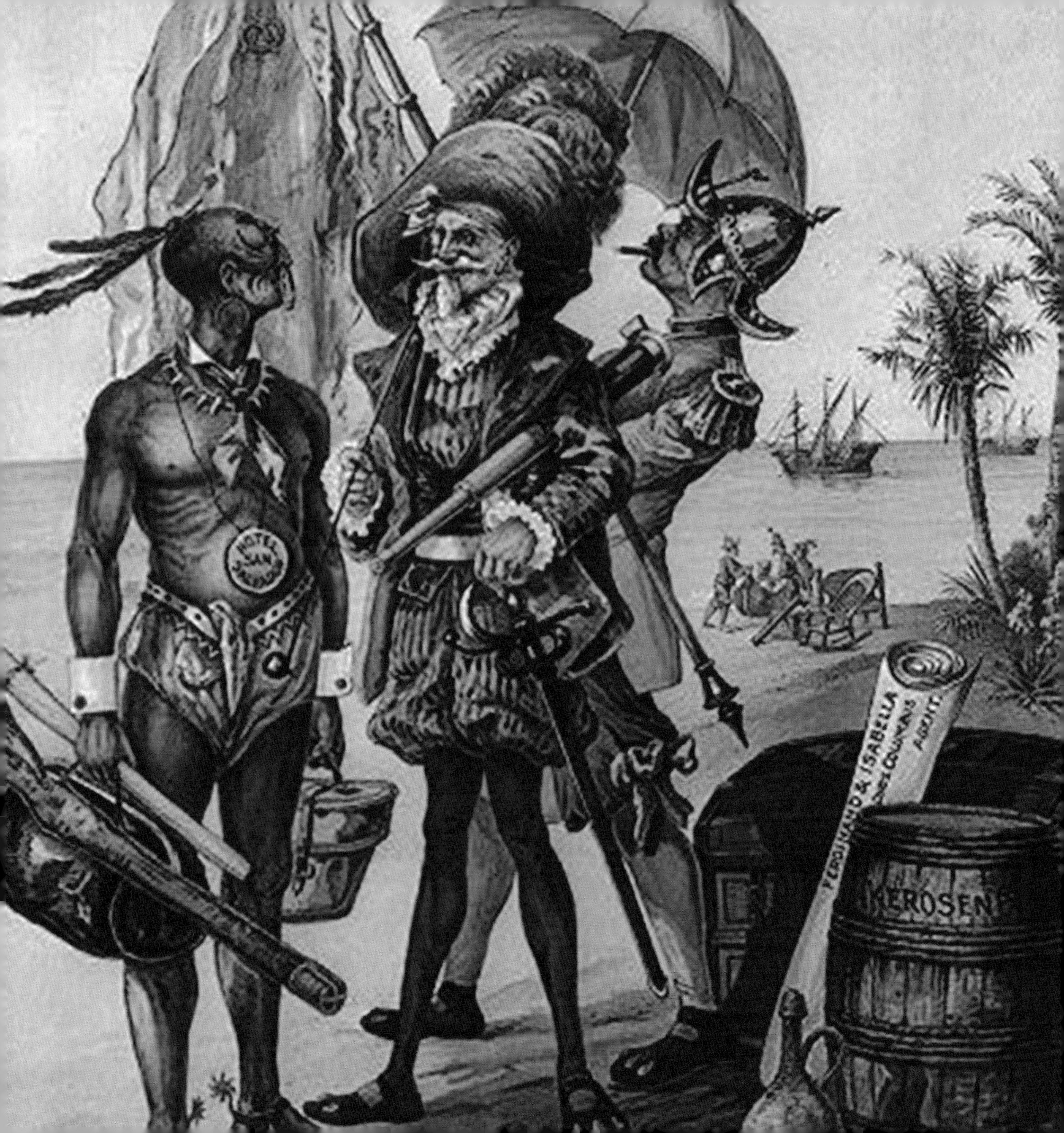
HOTEL SAN
FERDINAND & ISABELLA
KEROSEN

One of the greatest disasters resulting from the European arrival in and conquest of the New World was the destruction of many vibrant New World cultures. Some were lost so completely that we only know of them by reputation and legend.

For others we have the ruins of cities, complete with inscriptions on stones that we do not know how to read. Many Native American cultures continue, but in a much reduced way from what they might have been.

Columbus Statue

For the countries and cultures of Europe, access to the New World was a great challenge and a great gain. For the original people of the New World, the experience was almost completely negative and a disaster. This is why so many Native American have no interest in celebrating Columbus Day or honoring the explorer who "discovered" the New World in 1492.

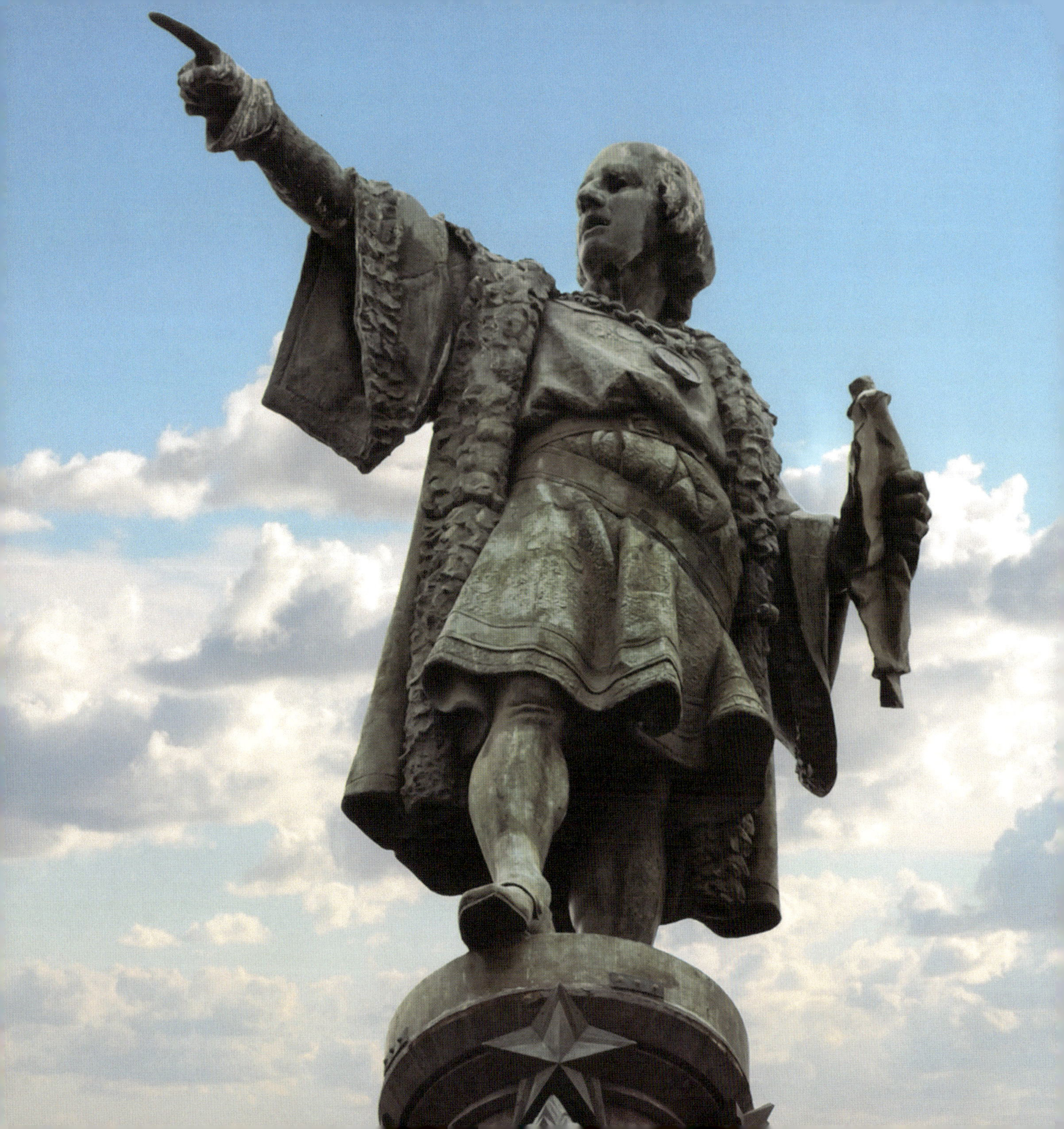

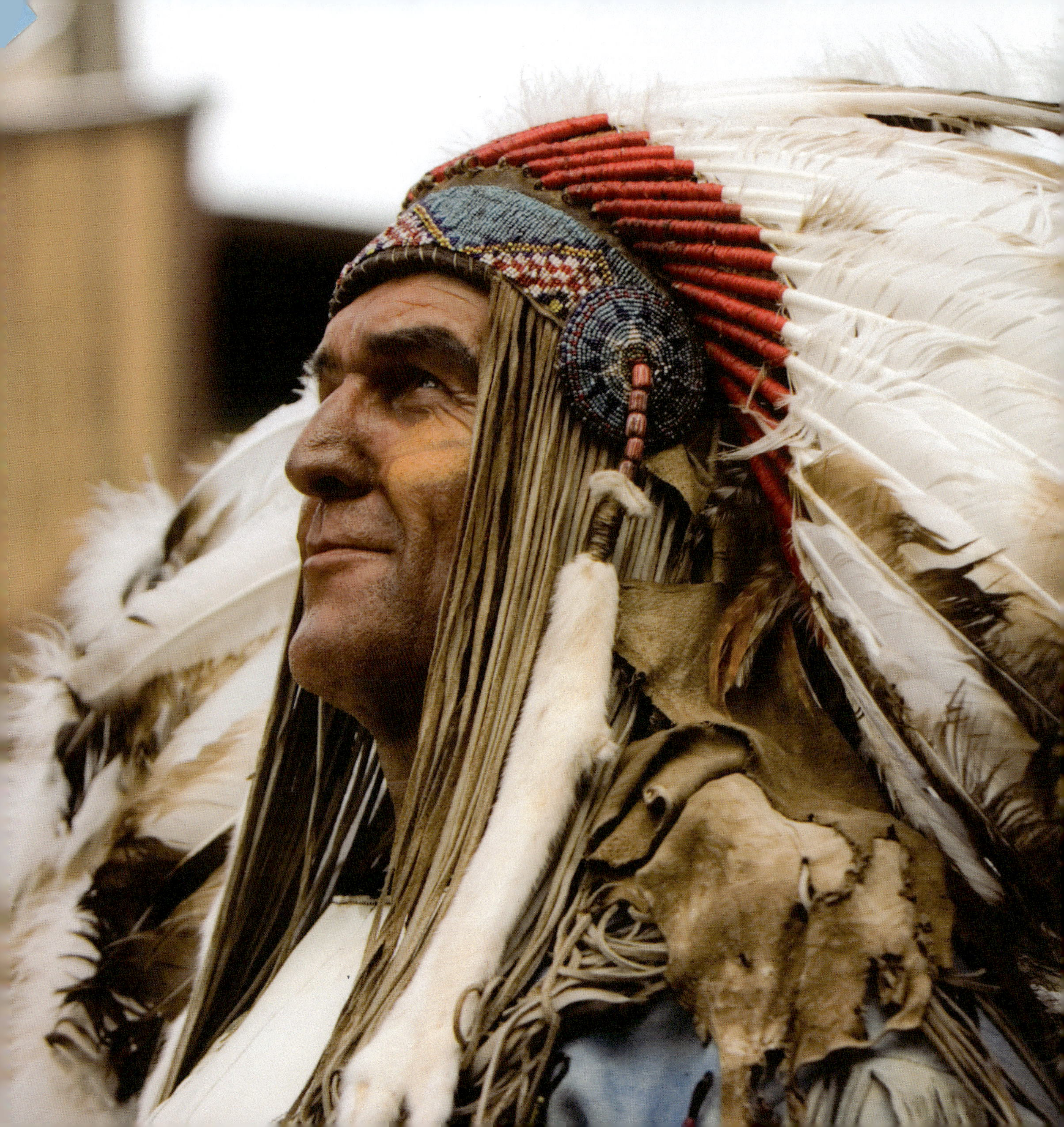

LEARN MORE ABOUT THE NEW WORLD

What were the Native American like before the Europeans got to North America? Find out more about their complicated and rich cultures in Baby Professor books like The World is Full of Spirits : Native American Indian Religion, Mythology and Legends and Getting to Know the Great Native American Tribes.

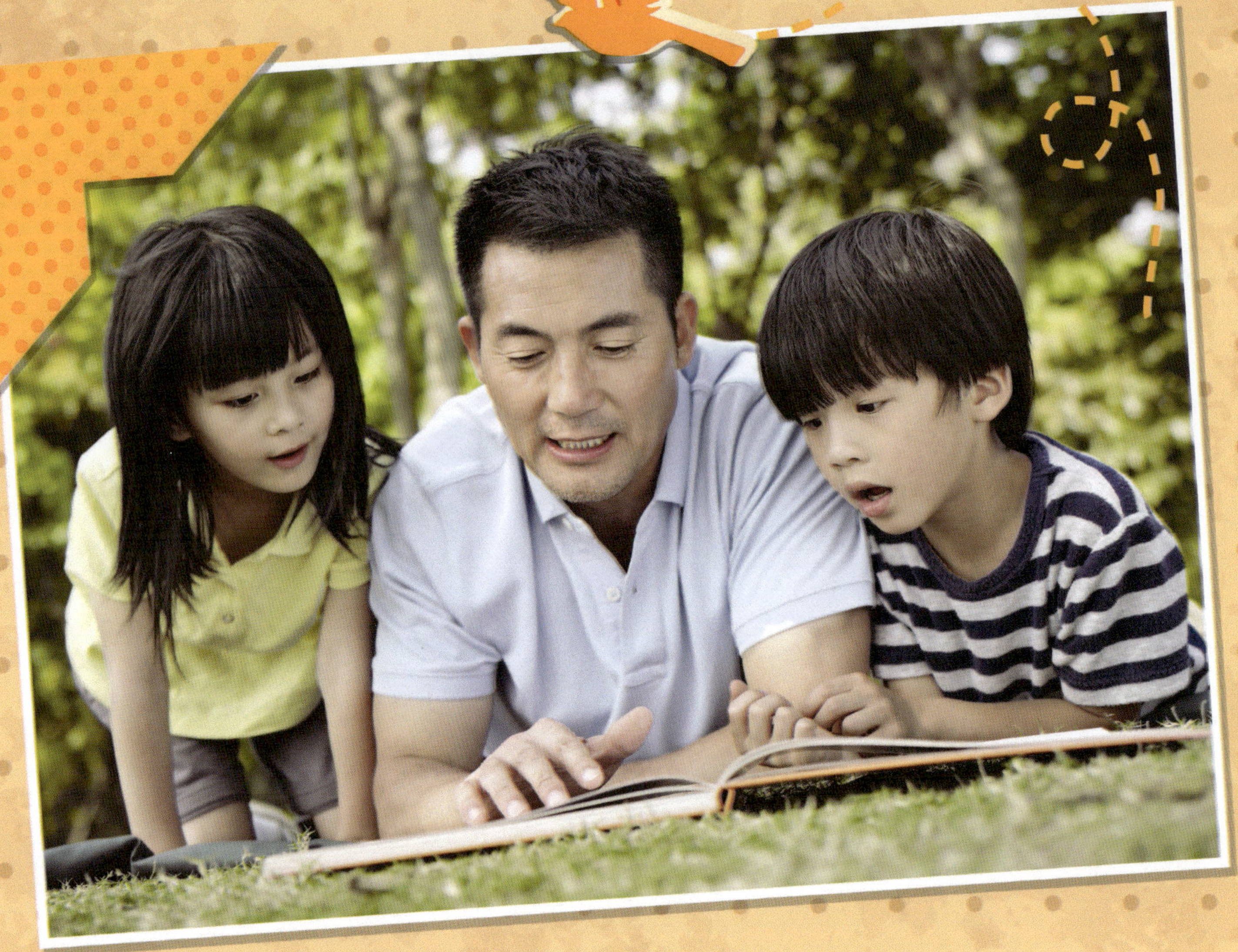

Visit

BABY PROFESSOR
EDUCATION KIDS

www.BabyProfessorBooks.com

to download Free Baby Professor eBooks
and view our catalog of new and exciting
Children's Books

Printed in Great Britain
by Amazon